THE FJH CLASSIC NOTE SPELLER
by Carol Matz

Production: Frank and Gail Hackinson

Production Coordinator: Philip Groeber

Editors: Victoria McArthur and Edwin McLean

Cover and Illustrations: Terpstra Design, San Francisco

Engraving: Tempo Music Press, Inc.

Printing: Tempo Music Press, Inc.

THE
F·J·H
MUSIC
COMPANY
INC.
Frank J. Hackinson

CONTENTS

Notes can be written by using small lines above or below the music staff, called **ledger lines**.

Ledger line notes above the staff:

Ledger line notes below the staff:

Outer ledger line notes are *above the treble staff* and *below the bass staff:*

Inner ledger line notes are *between* the treble and bass staffs:

In the diagram to the right, **notes on one ledger line** are shown.

Notice that from top to bottom, the notes spell **A C E**.

A ○ ← one ledger line above the treble staff

middle C ○ ← one ledger line below the treble staff *and above the bass staff*

E ○ ← one ledger line below the bass staff

The notes below are all on *one ledger line*. Write the letter name for each note (A, C, or E). Notice the clef signs.

Ex: _E_

___ ___ ___

___ ___ ___ ___

These are the letter names of the **treble clef outer ledger line notes:**

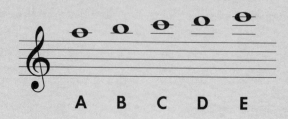

A   B   C   D   E

Look at the diagram below to see where these notes can be found on the keyboard.

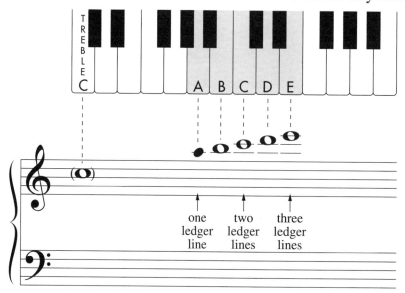

one ledger line   two ledger lines   three ledger lines

Remember that the note on one ledger line above the treble staff is **A** (from "ACE").
The next note up is B, which sits *above* one ledger line, then C on two ledger lines, etc.

To identify these ledger line notes, use the A as the "starting note," then think of the notes on two and three ledger lines as *skips* up from the A (every other key on the keyboard).
If a note is *above* ledger lines, it is one note (or a *step*) *higher* than the note *on* the ledger lines.

Ex: To identify think:
1. One ledger line is A ("starting note").
2. Two ledger lines is C (a *skip up* from A).
3. One note (a *step*) higher than C is **D**.

Write the letter name under each treble clef outer ledger line note.
(It may be helpful to find each note on the keyboard first.)

Ex: *E*   ___   ___   ___   ___   ___   ___   ___   ___

Write the letter name under each note below. (The letter names will spell words.)

_ _ _ _ _ _ M _ U _ _

_ _ T _ _ L _ I _ _ _

_ _ _ M _ W _ _ _

P _ _ _ _ N S _ _ _

Write a ledger line note above each letter to spell the words below.
Write half notes. (Make sure to draw down stems.)

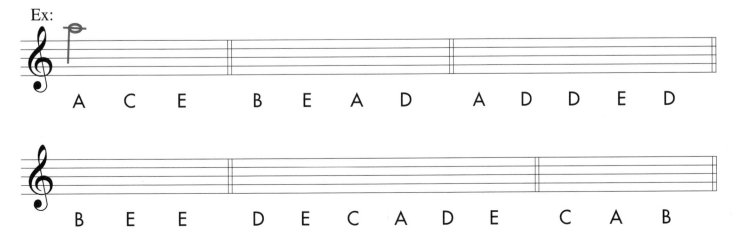

Ex:

A C E   B E A D   A D D E D

B E E   D E C A D E   C A B

These are the letter names of the **bass clef outer ledger line notes:**

Look at the diagram below to see where these notes can be found on the keyboard.

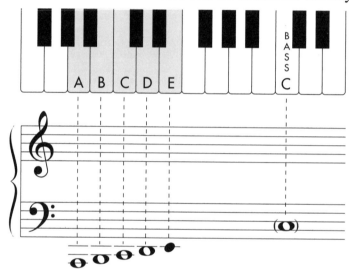

Remember that the note on one ledger line below the bass staff is **E** (from "ACE").
The next note down is D, which hangs *below* one ledger line, then C on two ledger lines, etc.

To identify these ledger line notes, use the E as the "starting note," then think of the notes on two and three ledger lines as *skips* down from the E (every other key on the keyboard).
If a note is *below* ledger lines, it is one note (or a *step*) *lower* than the note *on* the ledger lines.

Ex: To identify 𝄢 think: 1. One ledger line is E ("starting note").
2. Two ledger lines is C (a *skip down* from E).
3. One note (a *step*) lower than C is **B**.

Write the letter name under each bass clef outer ledger line note.
(It may be helpful to find each note on the keyboard first.)

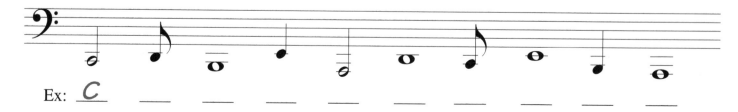

Ex: *C* ___ ___ ___ ___ ___ ___ ___ ___ ___

6

FJ

Write the letter name under each note below. (The letter names will spell words.)

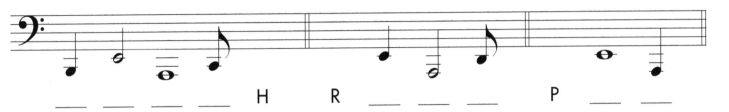

__ __ __ H R __ __ __ P __ __

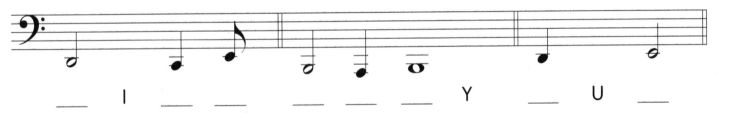

__ I __ __ __ __ __ Y __ U __

__ __ L __ N __ __ __ __ N __ __

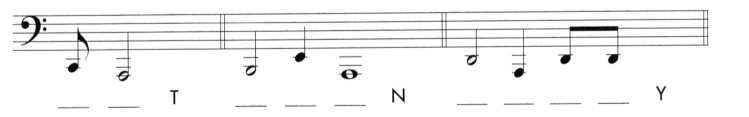

__ __ T __ __ __ N __ __ __ __ Y

Write a ledger line note above each letter to spell the words below. **Write whole notes.**

Ex:

C   A   B   A   D   D   B   E   A   D   E   D

D   E   E   D   B   E   A   C   E   B   E   D

Each grand staff below has both treble and bass clef outer ledger line notes.
Write the letter name under each note. (The letter names will spell words.)

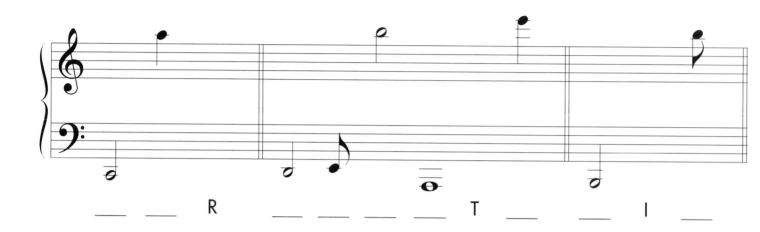

___ ___ R ___ ___ ___ T ___ ___ I ___

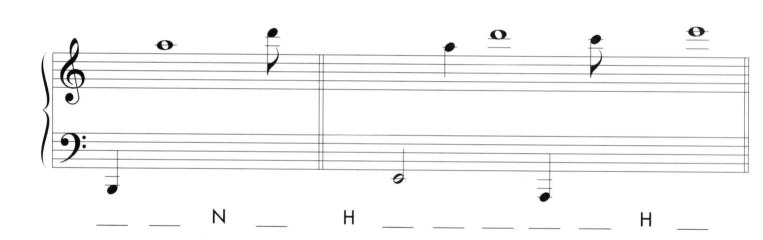

___ ___ N ___ H ___ ___ ___ ___ H ___

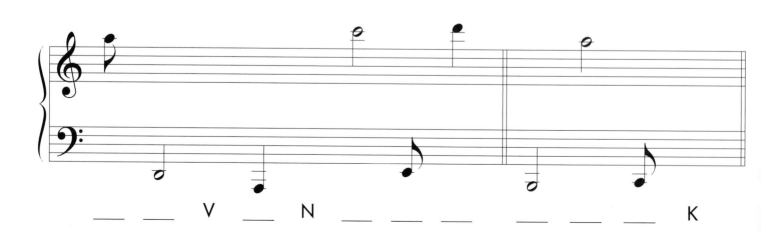

___ ___ V N ___ ___ ___ ___ ___ ___ K

8

Write a ledger line note above each letter to spell the words below.
Choose both treble and bass clef outer ledger line notes.
(See examples below to draw up stems and down stems correctly.)

Write quarter notes:

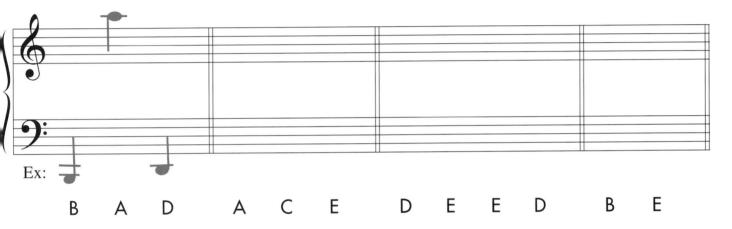

B A D   A C E   D E E D   B E

Write eighth notes:

C A B   D E C A D E   B E D

Write two ledger line notes (one on each staff) for the letter names given below.
Write half notes.

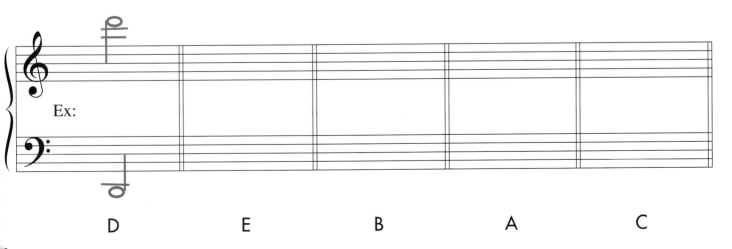

D   E   B   A   C

These are the letter names of the **treble clef inner ledger line notes:**

Look at the diagram below to see where these notes can be found on the keyboard.
Notice that the notes are below the treble staff. (All inner ledgers are *between* the two staffs.)

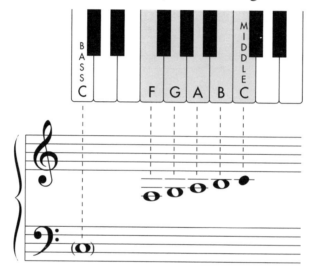

Remember that the note on one ledger line below the treble staff is middle **C** (from "ACE").
The next note down is B, which hangs *below* one ledger line, then A on two ledger lines, etc.

To identify these ledger line notes, use middle C as the "starting note," then think of the notes on two and three ledger lines as *skips* down from middle C (every other key on the keyboard).
If a note is *below* ledger lines, it is one note (or a *step*) *lower* than the note *on* the ledger lines.

Ex: To identify   𝄞   think: 1. One ledger line is middle C ("starting note").
                                                   2. Two ledger lines is A (a *skip down* from middle C).
                                                   3. One note (a *step*) lower than A is **G**.

Write the letter name under each treble clef inner ledger line note.
(It may be helpful to find each note on the keyboard first.)

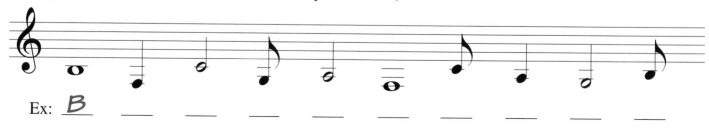

Ex: *B*   ___   ___   ___   ___   ___   ___   ___   ___

Write the letter name under each note below. (The letter names will spell words.)

___ ___ Y ___ ___ L ___ ___ U ___

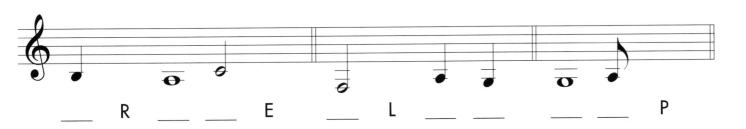

___ ___ P ___ R ___ ___ ___ ___ N ___

___ R ___ ___ E ___ L ___ ___ ___ ___ P

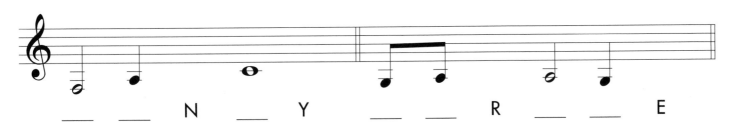

___ ___ N ___ Y ___ ___ R ___ ___ E

Draw an **X** through each ledger line note that is labeled incorrectly.

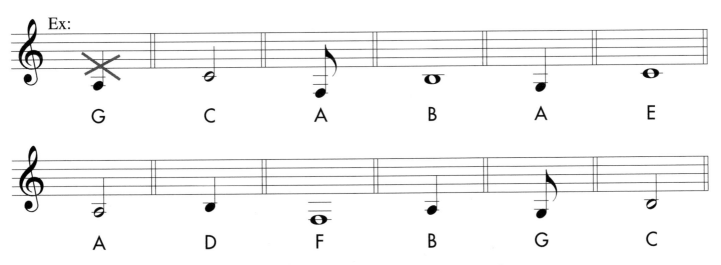

Ex:

G   C   A   B   A   E

A   D   F   B   G   C

These are the letter names of the **bass clef inner ledger line notes:**

C   D   E   F   G

Look at the diagram below to see where these notes can be found on the keyboard.
Notice that the notes are above the bass staff. (All inner ledgers are *between* the two staffs.)

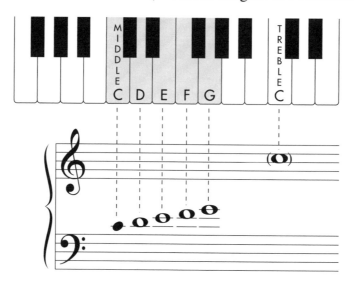

Remember that the note on one ledger line above the bass staff is middle **C** (from "ACE").
The next note up is D, which sits *above* one ledger line, then E on two ledger lines, etc.

To identify these ledger line notes, use middle C as the "starting note," then think of the notes on two and three ledger lines as *skips* up from middle C (every other key on the keyboard).
If a note is *above* ledger lines, it is one note (or a *step*) *higher* than the note *on* the ledger lines.

Ex: To identify 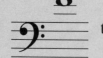 think: 1. One ledger line is middle C ("starting note").
2. Two ledger lines is E (a *skip up* from middle C).
3. One note (a *step*) higher than E is **F**.

Write the letter name under each bass clef inner ledger line note.
(It may be helpful to find each note on the keyboard first.)

Ex: *D* __ __ __ __ __ __ __ __ __ __

FJ

Write the letter name under each note below. (The letter names will spell words.)

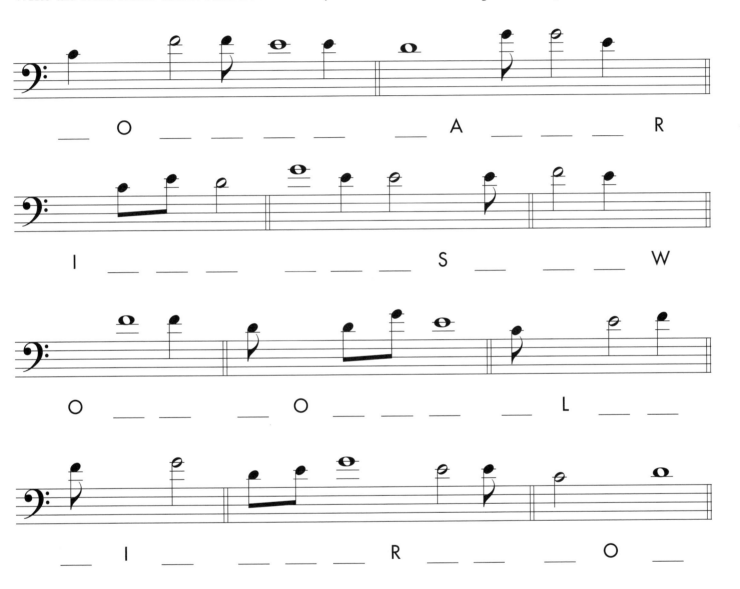

___ O ___ ___ ___ ___ A ___ ___ ___ R

I ___ ___ ___ ___ ___ ___ S ___ ___ ___ W

O ___ ___ ___ O ___ ___ ___ ___ L ___ ___

___ I ___ ___ ___ ___ R ___ ___ ___ O ___

Draw an **X** through each ledger line note that is labeled incorrectly.

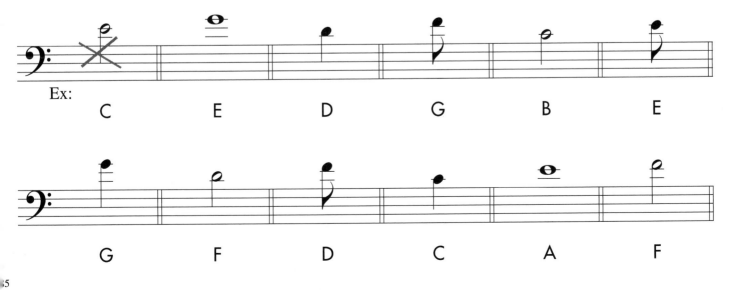

Ex:

C   E   D   G   B   E

G   F   D   C   A   F

Each grand staff below has both treble and bass clef inner ledger line notes.
Write the letter name under each note. (The letter names will spell words.)

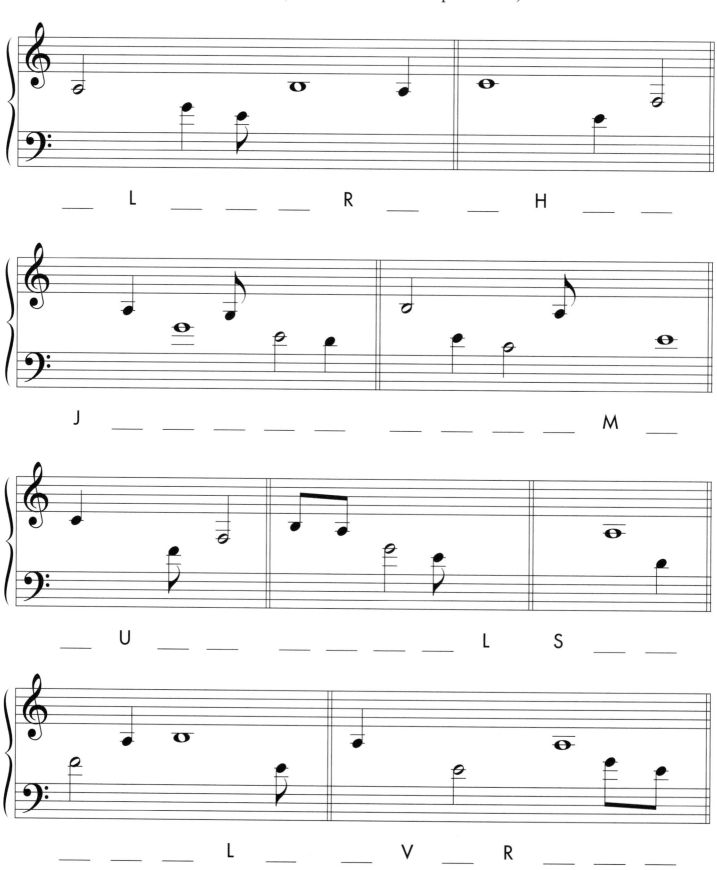

___ L ___ ___ R ___ ___ H ___ ___

J ___ ___ ___ ___ ___ ___ ___ M ___

___ U ___ ___ ___ ___ ___ L S ___

___ ___ ___ L ___ V R ___ ___

Write a ledger line note above each letter to spell the words below.
Choose both treble and bass clef *inner* ledger line notes.
(See examples below to draw up stems and down stems correctly.)

Write quarter notes:

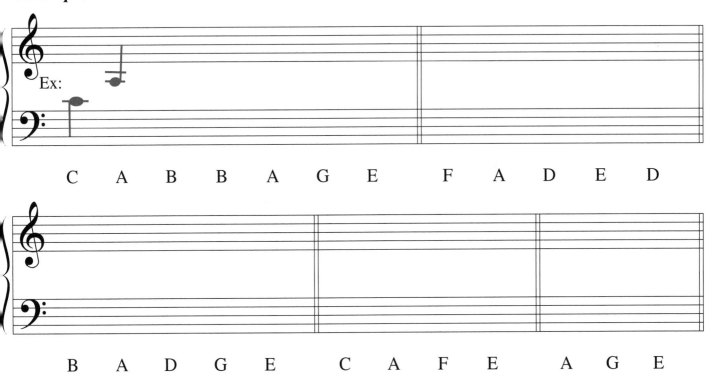

C A B B A G E F A D E D

B A D G E C A F E A G E

Write eighth notes:

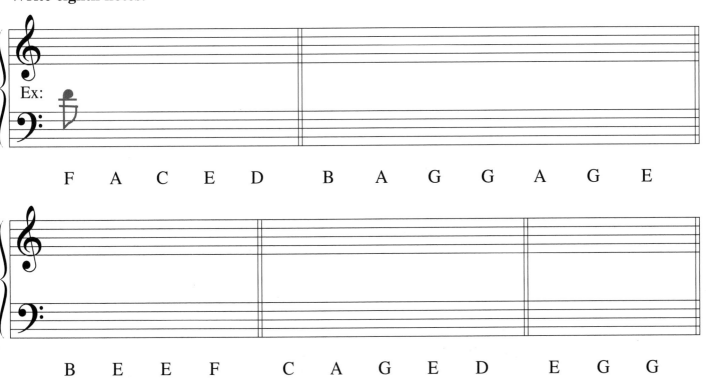

F A C E D B A G G A G E

B E E F C A G E D E G G

Each **inner ledger line note** can be written as a note in the *opposite clef.* The inner ledger line note and its matching note in the opposite clef stand for the same key on the keyboard.

For an example, look at the first diagram below: the F below middle C can be written in the treble clef (on 3 ledger lines) *or* in the bass clef (on line 4).

Treble Clef Inner Ledger Line Notes
(and their matching notes in bass clef)

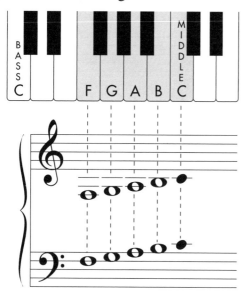

Bass Clef Inner Ledger Line Notes
(and their matching notes in treble clef)

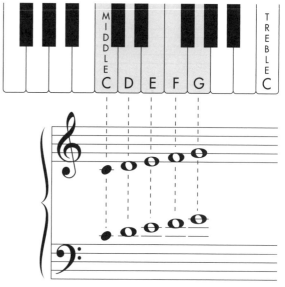

1. For each treble clef inner ledger line note, **write a matching note in the bass clef**.

2. For each bass clef note, **write a matching treble clef inner ledger line note**.

3. For each bass clef inner ledger line note, **write a matching note in the treble clef**.

4. For each treble clef note, **write a matching bass clef inner ledger line note**.

Look at the diagram below to review the location of the outer and inner ledger line notes.

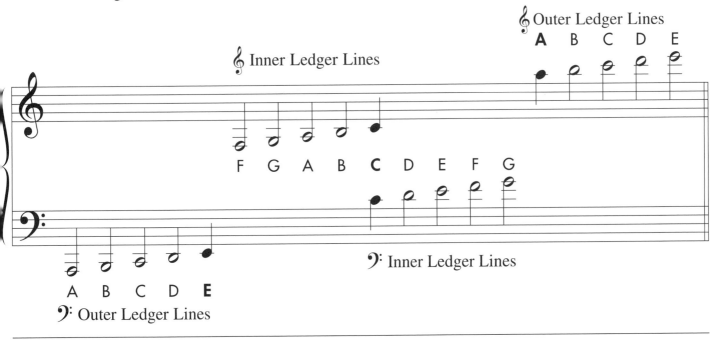

Draw an **X** through each ledger line note that is labeled incorrectly.

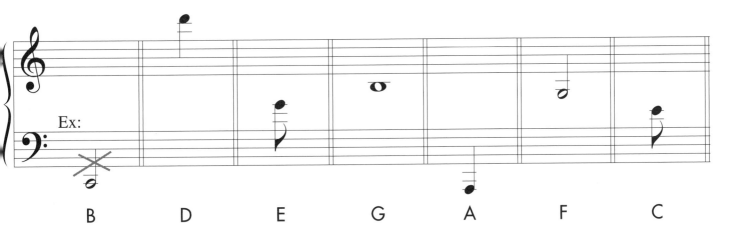

For each letter name given below, **write two more ledger line notes**.
Write whole notes.

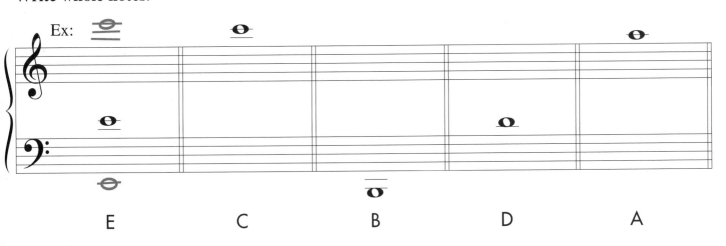

Each grand staff below has both outer and inner ledger line notes in both clefs.
Write the letter name under each note. (The letter names will spell words.)
Note: Remember the "starting notes" for one ledger line ("ACE").

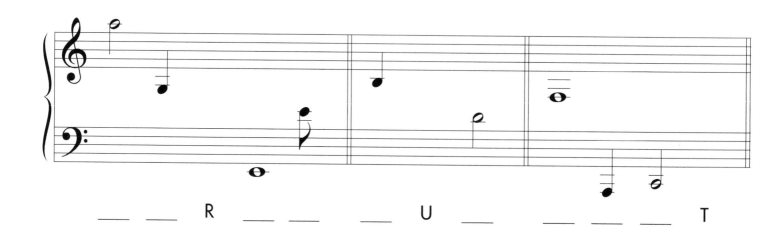

___ ___ R ___ ___ ___ U ___ ___ ___ ___ T

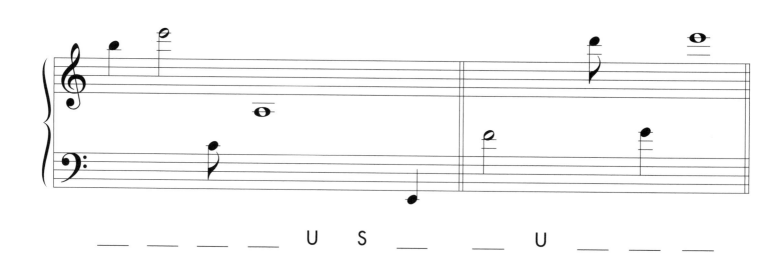

___ ___ ___ U S ___ ___ U ___ ___ ___

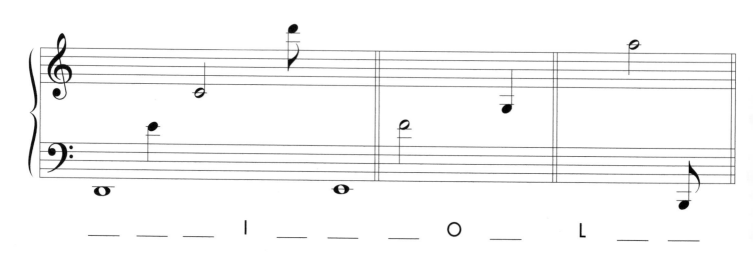

___ ___ ___ I ___ ___ O ___ L ___ ___

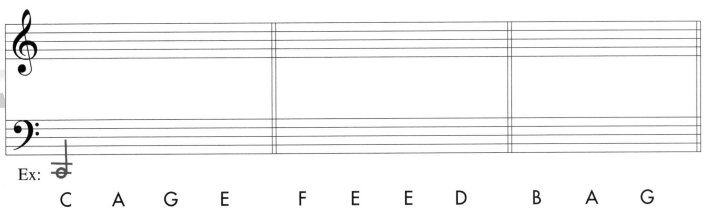

lesson 17 LEDGER LINE NOTE REVIEW, PART 3

Write a ledger line note above each letter to spell the words below.
Choose from all the ledger line notes you have learned.
(Use both treble and bass clef, outer and inner ledger line notes.)*

Write half notes:

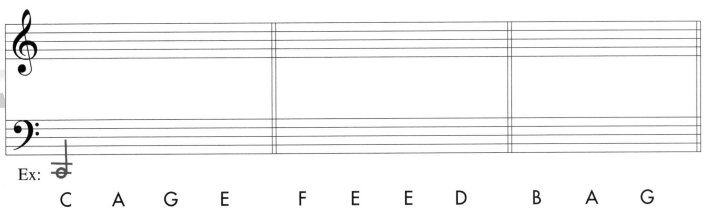

Ex:

C A G E   F E E D   B A G

Write whole notes:

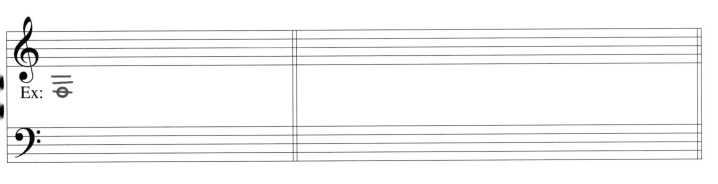

Ex:

F A D E   C A B   B A G E

Write quarter notes:

Ex:

E D G E   F A C E   B E E F

*Teacher's Note: If necessary, the student may refer to p. 33 for guidance on drawing the stems correctly.

Many times you will see sharps (#) or flats (♭) that appear after the clef sign at the beginning of each staff. This is called the **key signature**.

The key signature tells which notes are to be sharped or flatted *automatically* throughout the piece of music. (The sharp and flat signs *will not* appear in front of these notes in the music itself.)

The **key of C major** has no sharps or flats in the key signature. None of the notes in the music are *automatically* sharped or flatted.

The **key of G major** has an F# in the key signature. This means that *all* the F's (no matter where they are on the staff) are to be played as F#'s.

Key of C Major

Key of G Major

Each staff below has **F#** in the key signature *(the key of G major)*.
Write the letter name under each note. (The letter names will spell words.)
Remember to label all F's as F#'s. Notice the clef signs.

Ex: E   F#   ___   ___   ___   T   ___   O   ___   ___   ___

___   ___   N   ___   ___   S   ___   ___   ___   ___   R   ___   ___

O   ___   ___   ___   L   ___   L   ___

Key of F Major

The **key of F major** has a **B♭** in the key signature. This means that *all* the B's are played as B♭'s.

Each staff below has **B♭** in the key signature *(the key of F major)*.
Write the letter name under each note. (The letter names will spell words.)
Remember to label all B's as B♭'s. Notice the clef signs.

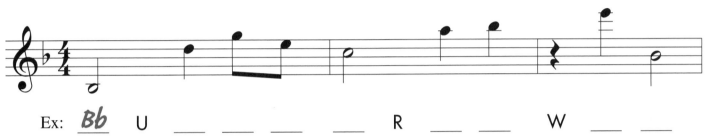

Ex: **B♭**   U ___ ___ ___ ___   R ___ ___   W ___ ___

___ ___ ___ ___   L ___ T ___ ___ ___ ___ ___ ___   Y

___ ___ ___ ___   T ___ I ___ ___ ___ ___ ___ ___   N

___ U ___ ___ ___ ___ ___   L ___ ___ ___   Y

Key of D Major

The **key of D major** has **F♯** and **C♯** in the key signature. *All* the F's and C's are played as F♯'s and C♯'s.

Each staff below has **F♯ and C♯** in the key signature *(the key of D major)*.
Write the letter name under each note. (The letter names will spell words.)
Notice the clef signs.

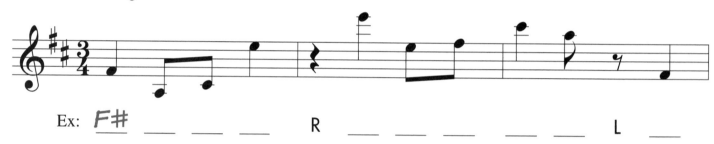

Ex: **F#** __ __ __ __ R __ __ __ __ L __

__ __ T __ __ __ __ U __ __

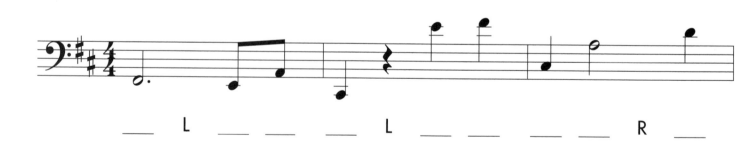

__ L __ __ __ L __ __ __ __ R __

__ R __ __ __ T __ __ __ N

Key of A Major

The **key of A major** has F♯, C♯, and G♯ in the key signature. *All* the F's, C's, and G's are played as F♯'s, C♯'s, and G♯'s.

Each staff below has **F♯, C♯, and G♯** in the key signature *(the key of A major)*.
Write the letter name under each note. (The letter names will spell words.)
Notice the clef signs.

Ex: *G♯* ___ ___ ___ T ___ ___ V ___ ___ ___ R

L ___ ___ ___ ___ ___ ___ ___ T ___ ___ S

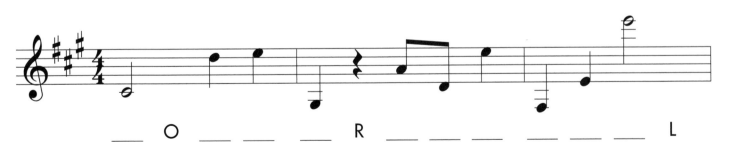

___ O ___ ___ ___ R ___ ___ ___ ___ ___ L

W ___ ___ ___ ___ ___ O ___ ___ Y ___ ___ N

23

Accidentals are sharp, flat, or natural signs *placed in front of notes in the music.*

Accidentals tell the musician to temporarily play these notes as sharps, flats, or naturals, no matter what is in the key signature.

Within the measure, notes found on the same line or space *after the accidental* are also changed.

Accidentals only "last" for one measure. In the example below, notice that the accidental had to be rewritten for the second measure of music.

F♯   also F♯

Write the letter name under each note below.
Watch for accidentals, and notice the clef signs.

Ex: _C_   _B♭_   _D_   _B♭_   __   __   __   __   __

__   __   __   __   __   __   __   __   __

__   __   __   __   __   __   __   __

lesson 23 | ACCIDENTALS, continued ♯ ♭ ♮

Sometimes you must watch for sharps or flats in the key signature *and* for accidentals:

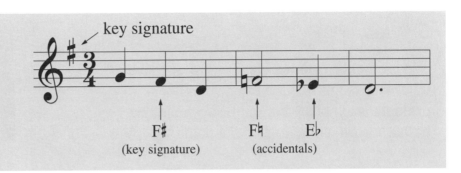

F♯
(key signature)
F♮   E♭
(accidentals)

The staffs below have sharps or flats in the key signatures, along with accidentals. Write the letter name under each note. Notice the clef signs.

Key of G major

Ex: **E♭** ___ ___ ___ ___ ___ ___ ___ ___ ___

Key of F major

___ ___ ___ ___ ___ ___ ___ ___ ___

Key of D major

___ ___ ___ ___ ___ ___ ___ ___ ___

Key of A major

___ ___ ___ ___ ___ ___ ___ ___ ___

The term **enharmonic** refers to two different letter names given to the same note. For example, each black key on the keyboard has both a "sharp name" and a "flat name."

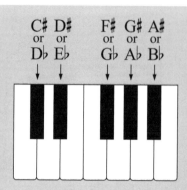

Example:

C♯ is the key nearest to the *right* of C.
D♭ is the key nearest to the *left* of D.

 C♯    D♭

C♯ and D♭ are enharmonic notes.
They are two different letter names for the same note (the same key on the keyboard).

In each diagram below, there is an arrow pointing to a black key.
Write two different letter names for this black key.

1.
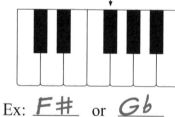

Ex: _F♯_ or _G♭_

2.
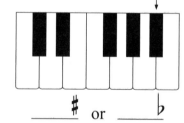

_____♯ or _____♭

3.
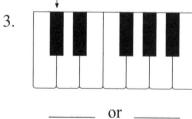

_____ or _____

4.
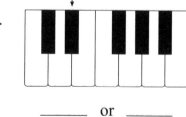

_____ or _____

5.
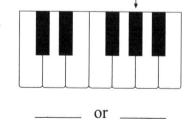

_____ or _____

6.
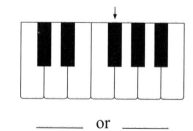

_____ or _____

lesson 25 ENHARMONIC NOTES, PART 2

For each sharped note given, write a flatted note (an enharmonic note).
Then write the letter names below each note.
(You may wish to refer to the keyboard diagram to the right.)

Ex: A# Bb   F# Gb   ___ ___   ___ ___   ___ ___

___ ___   ___ ___   ___ ___   ___ ___

For each flatted note given, write a sharped note (an enharmonic note).
Then write the letter names below each note.

Ex: Db C#   ___ ___   ___ ___   ___ ___

___ ___   ___ ___   ___ ___

The black keys on the keyboard are not the only notes to have enharmonic names.
Look at the diagrams below to see how some white keys can be named two different ways.

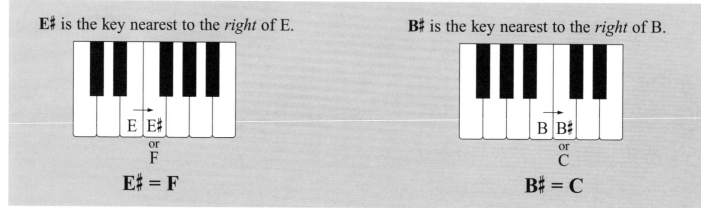

E♯ is the key nearest to the *right* of E.

E E♯
or
F

E♯ = F

B♯ is the key nearest to the *right* of B.

B B♯
or
C

B♯ = C

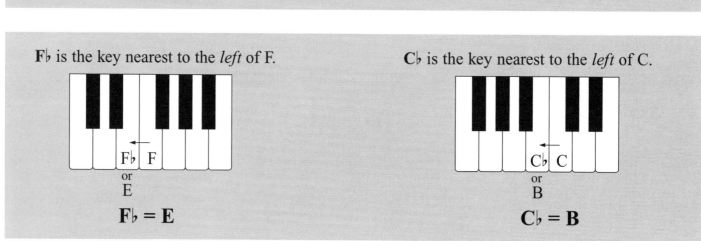

F♭ is the key nearest to the *left* of F.

F♭ F
or
E

F♭ = E

C♭ is the key nearest to the *left* of C.

C♭ C
or
B

C♭ = B

For each note given, write an enharmonic note. Then write the letter names below each note.

Ex: *B♯* *C* ___ ___   ___ ___   ___ ___

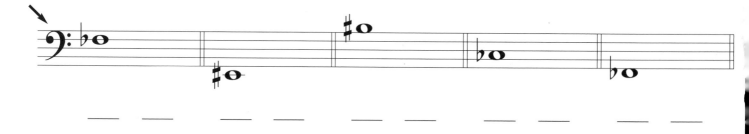

___ ___

Write an *enharmonic* letter name for each note below. (The letter names will spell words.)

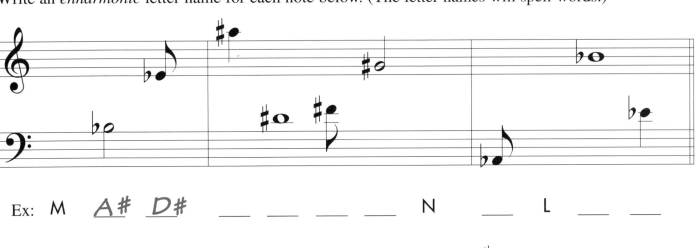

Ex: M   *A#*   *D#*   __   __   __   __   N   __   L   __   __

__   __   S   __   T   __   __   __   __   L   __

__   R   __   __   __   R   __   __   __   T

__   __   T   __   __   N   __   P   __   __

Review

1. Write the letter name under each ledger line note below.
   (The letter names will spell words.)

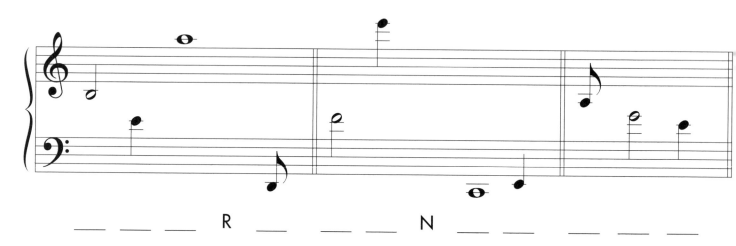

___ ___ ___ R ___ ___ ___ N ___ ___ ___ ___ ___

2. Draw an **X** through each ledger line note that is labeled incorrectly.

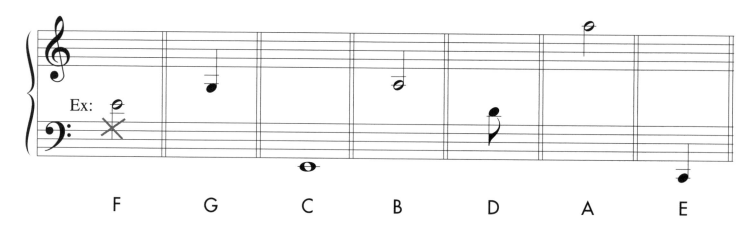

F   G   C   B   D   A   E

3. For each letter name given below, **write two more ledger line notes**.
   Write whole notes.

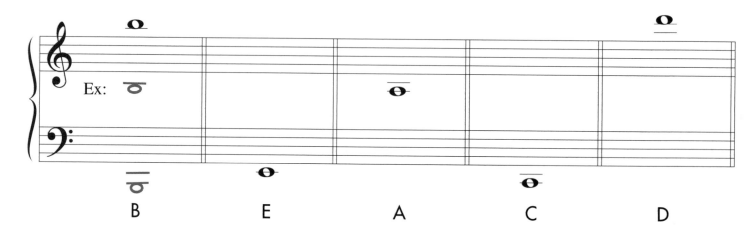

B   E   A   C   D

For each treble clef inner ledger line note, **write a matching note in the bass clef**.

5. For each bass clef inner ledger line note, **write a matching note in the treble clef**.

Draw a line connecting each key signature to its correct key name.

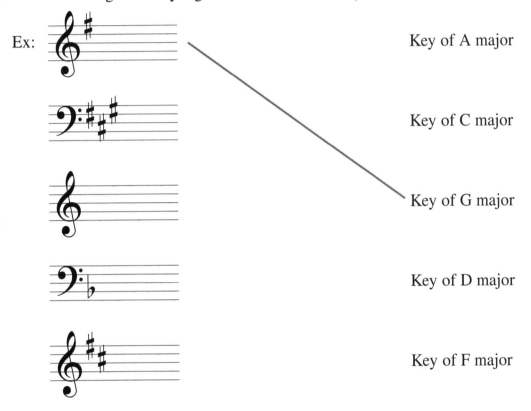

Ex:

Key of A major

Key of C major

Key of G major

Key of D major

Key of F major

Write the letter name under each note below.
Notice the key signatures, and watch for accidentals.

Key of F major

Key of A major

8. For each numbered black key in the diagram, write two different letter names in the spaces provided below.

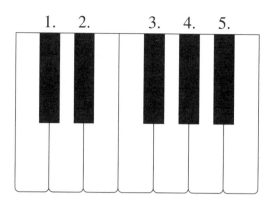

Ex: 1. _C#_ or _Db_

2. ____ or ____

3. ____ or ____

4. ____ or ____

5. ____ or ____

9. For each note given, write an enharmonic note. Then write the letter names below each note.

Ex: _Gb_ _F#_ ___ ___ ___ ___ ___ ___

___ ___

10. Write an *enharmonic* letter name for each note below. (The letter names will spell words.)

Ex: _C#_ ___ S ___ ___ ___ P ___ ___ ___